Norfolk Origins

1: HUNTERS TO FIRST FARMERS

Bruce Robinson
in collaboration with the Norfolk Museums Service

Archaeological Adviser: Andrew J. Lawson, Norfolk Archaeological Unit
Illustrations: Susan White and Denise Derbyshire

 ACORN EDITIONS

Dating

The following standard is employed:

BC represents approximate calendrical date.

b.c. represents radio-carbon date.

The scientific technique of obtaining dates from fossil charcoal, although invaluable, is now known not to be absolutely accurate. Radio-carbon 'years' are now known to be slightly different in length from calendrical years. For example, a date of 2000 b.c. (in radio-carbon years) might be recalibrated to circa 2500 BC. As this variation is still the subject of considerable research it is felt inappropriate at this stage to attempt to adjust radio-carbon dates.

Text and illustrations © Acorn Editions, 1981

ISBN: 0 906554 05 5

Published by Acorn Editions, Fakenham, 1981

Designed and produced by Sharp Print Management, Fakenham, Norfolk
Printed in Great Britain

Contents

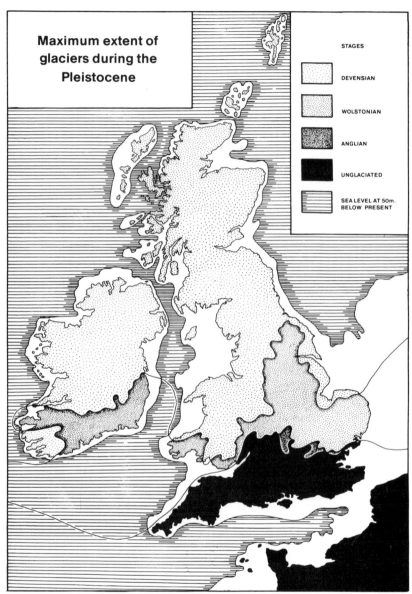

Fig 1. *Map of the British Isles* showing the maximum extent of glaciers at different stages of the Pleistocene Epoch. When the glaciers were at their maximum extent so much water would have been locked up as ice that the sea level would at times have been reduced much more than 50m. Hence for much of man's early history in Britain these islands would have been directly accessible from the Continent.

4

Introduction

In 1960 the late Rainbird Clarke's book on the archaeology of East Anglia was published. Since then it has been widely used as the textbook for the archaeology of the region. However, many of the concepts in that commendable publication have been superseded as a result of discoveries and research carried out in recent years. Our understanding of prehistory of the region has changed radically. Since the late 1950s with the widespread use of radio-carbon dating, the start of the New Stone Age has been pushed back from 2500 to 4000 BC. Even now for the earlier periods dating techniques are still inadequate; the arrival of man in our region can only loosely be put at about 400,000 BC.

Much has been written during the last 20 years, but most of it is in specialist literature not easily available to the general reader. There is now a great need for a new popular publication, particularly for interested adults and for older schoolchildren. We hope this book will satisfy that need, and if it does it will be followed by others covering the archaeology of the county through the Iron Age, Roman, Anglo-Saxon and later periods.

Since Rainbird Clarke was writing, the 1960s saw the advent in this region of large-scale rescue excavations making use of hired earth-moving equipment to excavate open areas. The introduction of open area excavations coupled with more realistic funding of field archaeology by central government has made it possible over the last 20 years to investigate extensive areas of sites which would previously have been examined in fairly restricted hand-dug trenches. Only a few sites have so far been dug in this way, but this technique as much as anything else will ensure that there will be, in the next 20 years, further significant improvements in our understanding of the history of man in the region.

Only a few large-scale excavations on prehistoric sites have yet been conducted in Norfolk, although some of these are notable. Revised ideas on the prehistory of the area have come from the study of collections principally of stray finds and sites and from comparison of these with excavated examples from outside the area.

More recently the 1970s saw the creation of county archaeological units; in Norfolk the Archaeological Unit is a department of the Norfolk Museums Service; in Suffolk it is a section of the County Planning Department. The Norfolk Unit along with the Archaeology Department in the Castle Museum in Norwich has charge of the county Sites and Monuments Record in which every known archaeological site, stray find or building of special interest is recorded. This is one of the oldest such records, actually started by Rainbird Clarke about 1930. This index is the main source for all archaeological research in the county. Additional information is constantly being put into this index as a result of the Unit's own air photography and site surveys.

Archaeology is not, however, just the prerogative of professionals. Impressive results have been obtained through the enthusiastic fieldwork of dedicated amateurs. In addition chance finds of great significance are frequently reported to the Norfolk Museums Service. Farmers and farm workers, building site workers, those involved in gravel extraction, road schemes, and even gardeners are likely at times to produce something for the archaeologist. Anyone with a sharp eye and a keen interest in the past can look out for artefacts and report the results to their local museum or to the Unit at Gressenhall. Whenever you make a find, please make a careful record of where it came from and then bring it in for identification and recording.

Anyone seriously interested in taking part in an excavation in the county can of course do so by contacting the Unit at Gressenhall. The Unit will also be glad to advise those wishing to do fieldwork in their own locality. Amateurs are encouraged to join NARG (the Norfolk Archaeological Rescue Group) and may do so through the Unit. A list of museums and sites to visit will be found at the end of this book (p.47).

We hope that readers of this new series will find the books stimulating and will be encouraged to take pleasure in studying the history of their landscape and the evidence for the people who have lived in it over several thousand years.

Peter Wade-Martins, County Field Archaeologist
Norfolk Archaeological Unit, Gressenhall, May 1981

Background

To begin at the beginning is more easily said than done, because the beginning is hard if not impossible to discern and the perspective of time difficult to grasp.

Distance, for example, is commonly experienced physically (walking or travelling) and mentally (map reading, perhaps); similarly, time is more easily amenable to the mind as well as to the senses once a familiarity, or a reference point, has been established. Despite this, the vastness of the Palaeolithic, or Old Stone Age (in East Anglia, perhaps more than 400,000 years) is still difficult to comprehend even when set beside, for example, the Roman period in Britain (about 400 years). As the late Roy Rainbird Clarke wrote in 1960, 'A scale of these dimensions reveals to the mind how long mankind has struggled in savagery and for what periods, in comparison, the states of barbarism and civilisaton have existed.'

The words 'savagery' and 'barbarism' and 'civilisation' are emotive and even arguable, but Clarke's central theme nevertheless remains true. Time out of mind is obscure, and becomes increasingly so the more it recedes into the past.

One way to try to grasp the problem is thus. Imagine the entire history of our planet condensed into a single century. In that case it is possible to suggest, though with no great degree of accuracy or certainty, that the oldest known rocks began to form at the dawn of year 15, that bacteria and algae appeared in year 26, that the first amphibians struggled ashore in year 92, that the dinosaurs were dominant in year 97 but were extinct in year 98, that man first walked upright three weeks ago, and that the last ice age ended a mere two hours ago.

Now try another reference framework. Imagine a one hour clock marked in sixty one-minute divisions. It represents time from the beginning of the Palaeolithic in our area, through to the present day, and it starts to tick at about 500,000 BC.

The remarkable fact is that something like 58 minutes of the hour would be used up simply 'time travelling' through the Palaeolithic. The 59th minute, roughly, would be taken by the Mesolithic (the Middle Stone Age), leaving a single remaining minute to accommodate the Neolithic (New Stone Age), the Bronze and Iron Ages, the Roman, Anglo-Saxon and Medieval periods and, in the final few ticks, Modern times.

The boundaries of man are not easily defined, either, and only now are we beginning to construct a picture of these early environments.

Although the environment was altered by man from the Mesolithic onwards it must, at times, have acted as a physical barrier, isolating one group from another though not necessarily, for example, separating Norfolk from what is now Suffolk. Nor is it possible to look at one group in isolation. The way one group reacts and develops is more often than not influenced by events and ideas from outside its geographical or social boundaries.

Thus this booklet, in attempting to describe Prehistoric Norfolk, would confine itself to the area within the county boundary only at the risk of presenting an unrealistic and incomplete picture.

In the same way that time and the passage of people and ideas blur man-made divisions, so it is that the invented labels applied to these divisions also become blurred.

The 'Three Age System' – the Stone, Bronze and Iron Ages – was a convenient sub-division of the human past, and indeed it still acts as an indicator of the technological ability of past populations. However, the transition from one 'Age' to another, though no doubt it had a major effect on every day life, may not have been as great an indicator of the replacement of one group of people by another as previously thought. The endings and beginnings of the periods and technologies that the labels indicate were not sharp-edged and sudden, but the result of slow transition and over-lapping processes which in some cases took many hundreds of years. Yet the labels remain because they are handy tools; no more, no less.

Most of Norfolk, and indeed much of East Anglia, lies below the 90m (300ft) contour and is thus usually described as 'low lying'. There are no mountains of folded or upthrust hard rock of a type which, in other areas, was used as a building material. Thus Norfolk has no durable monuments such as megalithic tombs or stone circles, and no cave paintings. Nevertheless, it still offers a more continuous sequence of history than many other parts of Britain.

Since 1960 (when Roy Rainbird Clarke published *East Anglia*) even more has been learned, and more human activity defined. This is due to an increase in the public awareness of antiquities, an increase in the number of professional archaeologists working in the area, and the development and refinement of many useful aids.

These include improved field techniques; metal detectors; tree-ring dating; fluorine testing (the dating of bones by measuring the amount of fluorine they have absorbed); carbon-14 dating (the measurement in dead organic matter of the radioactive isotope C-14, which disappears at a known and calculated rate); aerial photography; studies of the sea bed (which can show changing ocean temperatures); pollen and organic analysis; and palaeomagnetism (a study of changes in the earth's magnetic field).

For these and other reasons Norfolk's Sites and Monuments Record in 1980 contained details of over 16,000 sites and find spots. Many have been lost (erosion, damage, cultivation) while many other sites, no doubt, await discovery. For this reason, this account makes no claim to finality.

One effect of all this research and study is that the activities of man, and his time division indicators, are continually being amended and in the main pushed further and further back.

The watershed between the east coast rivers and the Wash rivers lies in an area of heavy soil chiefly derived from boulder clay. This wide tract divides the centre of Norfolk and Suffolk and formerly supported woodland which may have marginally impeded communication between the areas to the east and west. At one stage it was thought that primitive people lived largely on the fen edges west of the Icknield Way and on the chalk uplands, surrounded by impenetrable forest. It is now realised that the general distribution, though uneven, was much wider than that.

Another substantial feature of the area is a chalk ridge, five to ten miles wide and over 300m thick in places which, after the Neolithic period, probably formed a belt of relatively open country to the west of the boulder clay. This corridor, which passes through west Norfolk to reach the coast near Hunstanton, connects East Anglia with southern England.

Some of the geological regions and sub-regions were clearly more attractive than others to early visitors (because of the presence of rivers and water, the availability of materials and food, and the ease of tillage), but the precise relationship between human needs and man's immediate environment is still the subject of close and complex study.

However complex the pattern, the setting has remained far from static. It has been modified on one hand by human activity and on the other primarily by natural forces which have shaped and altered the landscape and its appearance by changes in climate and vegetation and the movement of land, sea and ice, which constantly enlarged or restricted those areas available for settlement.

The earliest dating for man associated with tools in Africa (Olduvai Gorge, 1.8 million years) has been pushed back several times in the last 20 years. For all that, the dating of man's first appearance in East Anglia, perhaps about 400,000 BC during the Palaeolithic, has remained at the same figure as that quoted by Clarke despite extensive attempts to pin-point local events more accurately.

Throughout this immense period, 50 times as long as the rest of human history, the area was in the intermittent grip of the ice. Indeed, on numerous occasions the climate altered so dramatically that glaciers invaded the territory from the west or north and then gradually melted or retreated, the intervals of glaciation, and the intervals between the advances, lasting thousands of years. It was a slow, cyclical process. At times, the 'interglacial' climate was warmer than we would experience today.

As the buried deposits of these stages are represented better in our region than elsewhere in Britain, many are named after sites (eg Paston, Beeston, Cromer, Ipswich, etc) whose names are familiar in East Anglia.

After the Cromerian interglacial stage (about 500,000 BC) came the Anglian glaciation which, being widespread, altered the landscape quite considerably; and which in turn was followed by the Hoxnian interglacial at about 350,000 BC. Then (c 225,000 BC) came the Wolstonian glaciation. The major effect of all this change was the smoothing down of the chalk and the depositing of wide tracts of boulder clay and gravel which covered the earlier rocks and former estuarine deposits. It also altered drainage patterns and largely dictated the basic shape – except the coastline – of the Norfolk countryside as we know it today. During the periods of extreme cold the sea level would have been reduced by more than 50m, the water being locked-up in ice in the glaciers. Even then, the Wolstonian was to be followed by the Ipswichian interglacial and, about 80,000 BC, by the Devensian glaciation.

About 8000 b.c. the last cold period of the Late Glacial phase – with its tundra conditions and birch copses – gave way to a milder climate, the local evidence for this coming from a study of pollen grains of trees and plants recovered from the peat and mud of the Fens, the Breckland meres, the north Norfolk coast and the Broadland valleys. Later, drier and warmer conditions triggered an expansion of pine and hazel. The birch was finally displaced by mixed-oak forest. Then an increasing wetness stimulated the development of the deciduous forest, which changed yet again when climatic conditions began to deteriorate. This time (in the Fens, for example) the woods gave way to expanses of sedge and shallow water.

Until about 6400 b.c. Norfolk was still united to the Continent, and at one time a coastline stretched from the present coast of Yorkshire round the Dogger Bank to join the western shore of Jutland.

The North Sea basin, once a land of forest, swamp and freshwater pools, finally succumbed to inundation. At several points off the Norfolk coast, particularly at Thornham, Titchwell and Sea Palling, the trunks and stools of these ancient trees can still be seen at low tide and remnants picked up on the beach. The moist, flaky pieces resemble wet peat, but when dry they become brittle and crumble. Pollen analysis suggests that the trees were growing c 5000 to c 2500 b.c. However, the finding at Thornham of a polished flint axehead embedded in a trunk, and other artefacts elsewhere, suggests that at least parts of the area were accessible during the Neolithic.

Towards the end of the Neolithic further extensive flooding led to the submergence of another large area off the north west Norfolk coast and, temporarily, what are now the Fens.

To conclude this brief background a few other points are also worth making.

Despite the many complex changes which overcame the peoples of different traditions throughout this long period of time, the most important advances in the Prehistoric era were basically three-fold. In general, the peoples of the Palaeolithic and the Mesolithic were the hunter-gatherers; Neolithic people were the first farmers. Thus the main advances might be described as economic (the beginnings of trade), technological (from stone to metal, from bronze to iron), and social (an enlarging and more settled population).

A land route of some importance lay along the chalk ridge where a series of tracks generically known as the Icknield Way indicates, roughly, a line of communication from beyond the Thames Valley to Hunstanton – though Hunstanton may not have been the original terminus – linking Wessex with East Anglia. Other trackways almost certainly existed.

Certain favoured areas of early settlement can also be discerned, and in many cases water and waterways were clearly influencing factors. Passage through the more thickly wooded areas was evidently achieved.

Finally, distribution and find-spot maps need to be interpreted with care. They simply indicate where artefacts have been found. Many artefacts may have been moved from their original resting place (by ice, or by cultivation); and, as many others are still waiting to be found it is not wise to draw too many conclusions from map clusters or gaps. Then again, and largely because of the tenacity of the soil and generations of cultivation, the heavier lands tend to produce fewer finds. Another influencing factor is an occasional concentration of archaeological or metal detector effort in specific areas.

Hunters (Palaeolithic)

Of the three major phases of glaciation it was the first, the Anglian, which proved the most widespread, the ice reaching as far south as the present Thames valley. The Wolstonian, from the north and west, reached almost as far, while the Devensian left the area south of the coast at Hunstanton largely unglaciated.

Even so it would be a mistake to think of Palaeolithic hunters in close contact with the ice fields. The existence of early man in the area was, by and large, restricted to interglacial periods when the ice had retreated north and when the climate, at times, may have been warmer than it is today.

For these reasons the most important evidence – worked flints – for the appearance of man in Norfolk and Suffolk is obtained from those deposits which were not destroyed by subsequent movements of the ice.

Worked flints recovered from cave sediments of late-Cromerian age near Westbury-sub-Mendip (Somerset) may provide the earliest record of human presence in the British Isles. They were first discovered in 1969 in a quarry on what is believed to have been part of a former cavern system. Five of the flints recovered showed apparent signs of workmanship. Two may belong to the Acheulian tradition.

The implication of the discovery, and several earlier discoveries, and its tentative pre-Anglian dating, suggests that man may have been present in southern England much earlier than at first thought. However, at the moment there is no incontrovertible evidence for any local East Anglian occupation prior to the Anglian glaciation – an epoch which terminated c 400,000 years ago on present assessment.

The bones and teeth of larger animals which earlier roamed the district are plentiful. For example, the freshwater deposits of the Cromer Forest Bed were formed in the delta of a river (perhaps the Rhine) into which were swept the remains of many species. It is clear that at this earlier time the climate was warm. Pollen grains and the remains of trees suggest areas of woodland, while in the marshes could be seen alder, pond-weed, sedge, water lilies, mare's-tail and many other flowering plants. And from Weybourne to Bacton and Corton to Kessingland have come the bones and teeth of the southern elephant, the Etruscan rhinoceros, hippopotamus, hyena, deer, horse and vole. But the notion of Palaeolithic hunters preying on this exotic game during the Cromerian and earlier stages is unproven. Man and his tools are conspicuous by their absence.

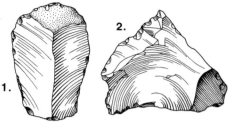

Fig 2. *Lower Palaeolithic Implements of Flint.* 1 & 2: simple utilised flakes from Clacton-on-Sea. 3 to 10: from Hoxne, Suffolk and including scrapers (3,4,5), a flake blade (6), a core (7) and hand axes (8,9,10).

The constant search for evidence of man's first arrival in the area explains to an extent some of the claims made for a series of flints recovered from the Suffolk Bone Bed and the Norfolk Stone Bed. They are often known as eoliths, or 'dawn stones'. They look convincing, but there are general objections to their acceptance as proof that man was living here before the Hoxnian interglacial.

Similar claims have been lodged for another 'industry', termed Cromerian, which consists of large flints of orange colouring from the Cromer Forest Bed. For the moment they are classified as of natural origin, produced by the battering of one pebble against another during water transport. Therefore, a projected date of c 400,000 BC for the arrival of man in the area is still accepted.

Flint tools are the main evidence of his presence. Their significance was not generally appreciated until 1797 when John Frere, squire of Roydon Hall, near Diss, suggested that some stone objects found at Hoxne (Suffolk) were implements belonging 'to a very remote period indeed; even beyond that of the present world.' His pronouncement, published in 1800, sparked considerable controversy and discussion. Since then, and because of the known succession of glacial and interglacial periods, East Anglia has been vitally important in the study of the Palaeolithic.

Despite Frere's discovery it is likely that the earliest tools were naturally fractured flints with sharp edges. By the time man reached Norfolk and Suffolk, however, he had developed a knapping technology. A first stage of human intervention would be to select a suitable flint and improve it by striking off small flakes from around the edges. A second stage of advance becomes evident when a flint object bears not only scars of random flaking but also a design from purposeful blows. The result is often a form which can be recognised. This in turn helps to divide

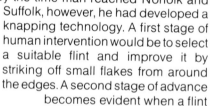

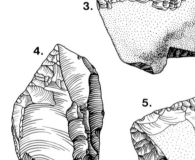

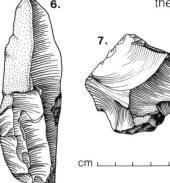

6.

7.

cm └─┴─┴─┴─┴─┘

the Palaeolithic very roughly into three phases: Lower (characterised by core tools), Middle (flake tools) and Upper (blade tools).

Three key East Anglian Lower Palaeolithic sites have been excavated in recent years, Clacton (Essex), Hoxne (Suffolk) and High Lodge, Mildenhall (Suffolk), a site which produced an assemblage dominated by hand-axes stratified above two earlier flake industries.

It becomes clear that the first securely dated human migration into East Anglia brought with it a method of working called chopper-core (or more recently, Clactonian, from the site where the tools were first recognised). These people lived between perhaps 300,000 and 400,000 years ago in what may have been a pre- or early temperate environment dominated by birch and pine trees.

9.

8.

The Clacton site produced the teeth and bones of straight-tusked elephant, fallow deer, rhinoceros, pig, horse, beaver and vole. It also produced flints discovered in the very position in which they had been discarded. They were in mint condition, and still sharp. The basic impression is of a crude, primitive industry, though there is no reason to think that Clactonian tools were any less effective than the more elegant artefacts of another over-lapping tradition, known as Acheulian (after St. Acheul in Northern France).

10.

This tradition is rather better represented than the Clactonian. Their wider selection of tools suggests a food gathering and hunting economy based on occupation sites – perhaps associated with broken woodland and grassland – often beside lakes or rivers.

Over 200 find-spots of Acheulian material have been recorded in Norfolk – only Kent and Hampshire having more – which have produced over 1200 hand-axes (the characteristic tool type) and 500 other tools, cores and flakes. Although large numbers of sites have been found only a few, in an industrial sense, seem to have been prolific. Virtually all of them are undated. They are assumed to be Hoxnian or Wolstonian because the majority of more accurately datable sites belong to these phases. But in view of discoveries such as Westbury-sub-Mendip (Cromerian) the matter remains uncertain.

Norfolk's Acheulian sites include Snarehill, Brettenham; Shrub Hill, Feltwell, which produced among other things over 230 hand-axes; Keswick (175 hand-axes); Kirby Bedon (Whitlingham), which had more than 200 hand-axes; South Acre; and Thetford.

Hoxne is the best local site to have produced refined hand-axes and delicate flake tools of the Acheulian tradition. Once again the tools were in mint condition, and micro-wear studies of the flints have shown they were used for many activities including adzing, boring, scraping, wedging, whittling, plant gathering or cutting, meat cutting, bone boring, hide cutting (the hide first being placed on a piece of wood, to enable an accurate cut to be made), which together suggests some sort of domestic industry based on wood or leather. Some of the later finds at Hoxne contained flake tools reminiscent of High Lodge, a site which dates from within the next cold phase.

At Hoxne, too, were found the remains of horse, red deer, bison, elephant, Macaque monkey, bird and fish, for as pollen analysis has shown mixed woodland certainly existed in the vicinity, though not necessarily as a vast forest. The site itself was beside a now extinct lake.

Hoxne also produced clusters of smashed bone, often horse, and some enigmatic stone clusters at the edge of the lake. These clusters could be regarded as some of the oldest archaeological structures in the region, even if their exact purpose is unknown.

What is clear is that the tools themselves were knapped from flints taken from outcrops of chalk or from earlier glacial beds. Then smaller shallow flakes were knocked off the surface by blows from a bone or wooden bar, thus producing a core tool. Waste flakes were often trimmed and used, the smaller probably as knives, the larger converted into cleavers with an axe-like cutting edge. A part of man's time, however, must have been spent in the manufacture of wooden artefacts which, along with the living shelters, have been lost because these organic materials naturally decay.

Population during the Clactonian and Acheulian periods was small despite the collective existence of hundreds of tools. Two things point to a sparseness of occupation. One family would be quite capable of producing several hundred flint tools in several days; and indeed, they probably needed to, for flint blunts very easily especially when butchering after a kill. A second point is that tools found so far represent tens of thousands of years of occupation. So it does seem that during the Hoxnian interglacial East Anglia was occupied by family groups each inhabiting tracts of landscape across which they followed the seasonal movements of the game.

What were the Hoxne lakeside dwellers like? It is impossible to say, for the evidence is slender or, in many respects, non-existent.

In general the people of this period are thought to have lived in family groups of perhaps a dozen or so men, women and children. Maturity seems to have been reached early and they probably died at what we would describe as a fairly young age. Even so, there is no reason to suppose they were not fit, generally healthy and usually happy.

They seem to have been short and slightly stocky in build. It is not known what they wore, or indeed if they wore anything. It is known, however, that they made use of skins and pelts – at least, they treated and scraped them – but whether the skins were then used as robes or shawls, tents or windbreaks, is uncertain.

Nothing is known, either, of the social organisation of these family groups. Each group presumably had a leader, but it is a matter of guesswork how the communal tasks were shared.

No doubt at their camps there was some debris lying around (the soles of the feet can harden to a quite remarkable degree) but it should not be assumed that living conditions were squalid. Nor should it be assumed they spent their leisure time sitting by the family fire. While some sites have yielded evidence of fire (charcoal, which could have been the result of accidental fire), there is no evidence of the use of hearths in Britain, although at this time they are known from elsewhere in Europe and Asia.

There is little doubt that activities at the hunter-gatherer stage of development were largely controlled by the environment. Dwelling sites were often restricted to the fringes of the forests or to locations beside the water. Seasonal movements of animals determined the duration and form of settlement in some areas, but man was already beginning to manipulate – if only on a small scale – some elements of the habitat. With tools (and possibly fire) at his disposal, he must also have gained an intimate knowledge of flora and fauna.

Once more, however, the climate grew cold as the ice sheets of the Wolstonian glaciation advanced over Norfolk from the north-west (c 250,000 BC). It forced the Acheulian hunters to retreat south, following the animals on which they depended. Thus for about 100,000 years the tundra was left to the woolly rhinoceros and the mammoth.

Fig 3 (over). *Reconstruction of a Lower Palaeolithic Campsite during the Hoxnian Interglacial (c.300,000 BC)*. Campsites, such as that recently excavated at Hoxne, Suffolk, were situated next to lakes or rivers. The warm summer climate promoted the growth of a rich forest broken by tracts of grassland on which herds of animals grazed. Many of these animals, such as the straight tusked elephant, rhinoceros and wild horse, are extinct in Britain today, but at that time were hunted by early man both for food and skins. Skins, amongst other things, were prepared with the help of knapped flint implements. It is probable that temporary shelters were erected for protection from the wind and rain, for although clothing and pelts were probably worn, there is little certain evidence that fires could be lit for warmth and cooking. Food, which included gathered fruit, nuts and roots, was eaten raw.

1.

cm └──┴──┴──┴──┴──┘

Fig 4. *Middle and Upper Palaeolithic Flint Artefacts.* 1: Middle Palaeolithic hand-axe from Little Cressingham. 2: Upper Palaeolithic tanged points from Cranwich. 3: Upper Palaeolithic blades, scrapers and core from Sproughton, Suffolk.

The warmer period which followed (the Ipswichian interglacial) may have had summers warmer and winters drier than today. On the open grass-lands, if people did return, they would have encountered elephant, rhinoceros, bison, herds of horses and the occasional lion; while in the woods lurked aurochs, deer, bear, pig and wolf; and in the ponds, the freshwater tortoise, frog and water vole. In some respects, at least, the way of life for returning hunters may have been similar to that of their predecessors. However, for some reason traces of man in the Ipswichian interglacial are almost totally absent.

The Devensian glaciation, which reached no further south than Hunstanton, nevertheless saw the ice advancing and retreating several times. To the 'Hunstanton advance' is attributed the deposition of the reddish-brown boulder clay recognised along a coastal strip of north-west Norfolk.

This was the framework of the Middle and Upper periods of the Palaeolithic, none of which is particularly well represented in terms of discovered artefacts. Of the later stages of the Acheulian or Mousterian (after Le Moustier, a rock shelter in the Dordogne) industries, some of which may be early Devensian, only three hand-axes are known from Norfolk – from Mousehold Heath (Norwich), North Wootton, and a more recent discovery at Little Cressingham.

In the 1970s two hand-axes and a flake were found on the bank of the Blackwater stream in that parish, the hand-axes being of a type usually found with Mousterian-like Levalloisian industries. No other undisturbed site of this early Devensian stage is known in the county.

2.

It seems that survivors of the Acheulian tradition were still making the hand-axe, but now it was thinner. smaller, often heart-shaped, and made from flake rather than a nodule.

18

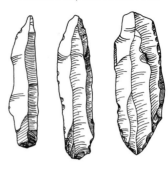

Other groups developed distinctive techniques of their own, one being known as the Levallois technique. A flake was evidently shaped while still attached to the parent nodule and was removed from the core, ready for use, by a bone or wooden punch hit by a wood or stone hammer.

Some scant evidence of the Upper Palaeolithic occupation has emerged during the last few years. A leaf point was found at White Colne (Essex) beneath a later Mesolithic site, and associated with mammoth; another site (including tanged point, scrapers and leaf points) was discovered at Bramford Road, Ipswich (Suffolk); Cranwich and Hockwold-cum-Wilton (both Norfolk) have produced flints and tanged flakes (which may be Late Upper Palaeolithic); and a flint industry site at Sproughton (Suffolk) produced two barbed points of antler and bone. The bone point was recovered above layers from which twigs and leaves gave dates of 11,940–11,370 b.c.

3.

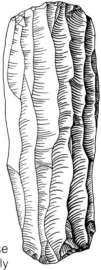

Whether man did keep his distance during the late Devensian period, as at first thought, now seems doubtful. In any event bands of hunters roaming Wales, south-west England and the southern Pennines can be detected. If he did inhabit Norfolk at this time, even during the slightly warmer phases between the periods of intense cold, the area would not have presented a particularly hospitable face to the wanderer.

For reasons already mentioned distribution maps can be misleading. They represent the relics of groups of hunters and incidental losses of tools spread over hundreds of thousands of years. Attempts to evaluate in detail the distribution is also made more difficult by a lack of knowledge of the topography of each precise locality during the interglacial periods. Nevertheless, and with some exceptions, a majority of Palaeolithic finds do seem to come from the valley gravels – washed there by melt waters – from the Norwich area, the lower Waveney valley, the Ouse, Thet, Wissey and Lark valleys in Breckland, and the Gipping valley.

A few human bones, but no skeletons, have been found in Britain throughout the Palaeolithic, which explains why guessing at man's actual physical appearance is such a hazardous business.

Micro-Technology (Mesolithic)

The next phase, the Mesolithic, represents comparatively few ticks of the time clock, and once again it was a period of slow transition and over-lapping traditions. This makes its origins and development difficult to trace. Despite this, and a sad shortage of datable materials and site plans it was, nevertheless, a significant period. Indeed, it might be said that within the Mesolithic can be perceived the seeds of present day society and perhaps the beginnings of East Anglian originality.

About 8000 b.c. the cold climate of the Late Glacial evolved into milder though still cold conditions, and it is this period, ending c 4000 b.c., which encompasses the Mesolithic.

The period began with a slow rise in temperature to an average of about 12°C in the summer – or a peak of about 2½°C lower than the average July temperatures we would expect now. Gradually the dwarf birch and willow copses of the tundra were replaced by woodlands of birch and pine. The mammoth and the woolly rhinoceros had retreated, or become extinct, but herds of reindeer at first survived, together with arctic hare, fox and white grouse. Later, with the spread of woodland, came aurochs, giant Irish elk, red deer, wild pig, wild cat and badger, to name but a few well authenticated examples.

Eastern England, of course, was still joined to the Continent, and much of what is now the southern North Sea remained freshwater fen and lagoon providing, for hunter-fisher communities, a potentially rich food source.

As already stated, Upper Palaeolithic hunters left behind comparatively few traces. Their successors, the Mesolithic, are equally elusive in archaeological terms. Palaeolithic survivors were probably joined by fresh groups from the Continent, perhaps coming across the land bridge from Denmark and the Baltic; but there is no evidence of a definite migration. Rather, it seems to have been a slow drift of people searching, no doubt, for new hunting grounds among the changed fauna and forest.

In general the Mesolithic may be divided into two phases, Early and Late. The first may be represented by communities at sites such as Kelling Heath, Lackford, Wangford (Lakenheath) and Colne Valley (Essex), while the later Mesolithic is best represented by finds from Peacock's Farm (Shippea Hill). Evidence of human occupation in East Anglia during the Early phase (c 8000 to c 6500 b.c.) is, however, irrefutable.

Birch no doubt remained abundant and hazel became more evident, while alder and mixed-oak forest began to colonise the heavier soils. At this stage Britain was still open to the direct influences of Denmark, southern Sweden and north Germany, but rising sea levels (due to the final melting of the frozen areas further north) gradually gained mastery and by c 7000 b.c. much of this 'Northsealand' plain was submerged. Even so, it would be another thousand years before Britain could be described as an island.

Confirmation of man's presence in the 'Northsealand' area first came in 1931 when the Lowestoft trawler Colinda was fishing between the Leman and Ower banks some 25 miles north-east of Cromer. During fishing operations she dredged a lump of peaty material called moor-log from a depth of about 35m. When it was dumped on deck out fell a barbed bone point of red deer antler.

Comparisons with similar objects from the Baltic make it clear it is the prong of a hunting spear. Scientific study has suggested it may be dated to c 7000 b.c., but the manner in which it was found leaves the precise dating open to question. Other examples of barbed bone point have been discovered at Sproughton (Suffolk), and elsewhere, and more recently at Feltwell. Flint implements, meanwhile, have been found in large numbers at Kelling Heath, in north Norfolk, Wangford, and at Lackford (Suffolk).

The sites yielded small, narrow flint blades, the waste products of knapping, and the rarer, modified blades or microliths. These could have been set in wooden hafts and used for cutting or boring. In reality, the range of functions of microliths is not fully understood. Some could have been used as missile points, while others seem too flimsy. Another suggeston is that microliths may have been used as parts of composite tools used in the harvesting of plant foods.

cm

Scrapers, borers, burins (small chisels) and core axes with cutting edges produced by detaching a transverse or 'tranchet' flake, also formed an integral part of the industry. One implication of the tools is that these groups were making use of timber. Indeed, pollen analysis of contemporary sediments – as for example, at Hockham Mere – indicates a disturbance of the forest edge, while Star Carr (Yorkshire), the most famous British site of the period, shows prepared wooden platforms.

Although there is no evidence for the construction of substantial dwellings it is possible that flimsy shelters were erected, for White Colne (Essex) produced evidence of irregular shaped dwellings, perhaps roofed with

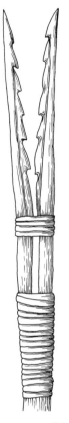

Fig 5. *Early Mesolithic Barbed Bone Points*. The examples (left) are from the Leman and Ower banks, off the north Norfolk coast, and Feltwell. The reconstruction (right) shows how two points were sometimes mounted together to catch fish or eels. (Also see title page)

1.

Fig 6. *Mesolithic Flint Implements.* 1: Tranchet axe from Lynford. This would have been hafted into a wooden handle. 2. Quartzite perforated pebble probably used for weighting a digging stick. 3: Early Mesolithic microliths from Kelling and how they were produced from a small blade. 4: Blades and cores from Wangford, Suffolk. 5: Late Mesolithic geometric microliths from Wangford, Suffolk and reconstructions (not to scale) of a few ways in which such microliths were mounted to form composite tools for reaping, hunting or sawing.

boughs and sod, and suitable for three or four people. Two pits, 2.5m across and 100mm deep, had been scooped out of the gravel, with a small hearth between.

The largest Early Mesolithic site known in East Anglia is Kelling Heath, which is now encroached upon by a caravan site. Set on a high, sandy heathland it gives evidence of a series of occupations and a wide range of implements possibly made from quarried flint. Lackford, a smaller site, produced cores, scrapers and microliths and a general technology largely identical to Kelling. Indeed Lackford, due to a less advanced type of microlith, may be the earliest Mesolithic site known in East Anglia, with Kelling second, but a shortage of datable material makes the matter uncertain.

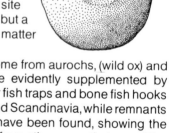

2.

The bulk of their foods seems to have come from aurochs, (wild ox) and deer, while in some areas supplies were evidently supplemented by fishing. Fishing nets with bark floats, wicker fish traps and bone fish hooks are known from elsewhere in the country, and Scandinavia, while remnants of dug-out canoes and wooden paddles have been found, showing the exploitation of inland waters. We also know from other areas that one of the dominant characteristics of Mesolithic traditions was the use of bone, but the finds of such objects are not widespread.

What is clear is that in the Late Mesolithic some tools were influenced by developments from the south (previously known as Sauveterrian), a tradition characterised by an absence of axes, adzes and similar equipment. Instead, they produced very small microliths of geometric forms like

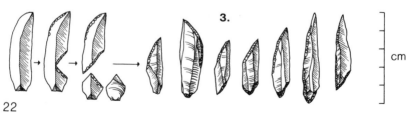

3.

cm

trapezes, crescents and triangles which were attached to darts and spears. Some of the microliths are beautiful and minute, as small as half an inch, and they demonstrate a high degree of manufacturing skill.

Traces of this tradition have been found at sites on the sand dunes bordering the Fens, as at Wangford, Plantation Farm and Peacock's Farm (Shippea Hill), and at Two Mile Bottom. The important Peacock's Farm site revealed a sequence of Mesolithic, Neolithic and Bronze Age layers in the peat beds suggesting the recurrent – though not necessarily continuous – occupation of a favoured site on a dry, sandy ridge over many hundreds of years.

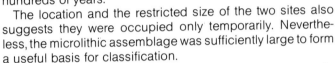

4.

The location and the restricted size of the two sites also suggests they were occupied only temporarily. Nevertheless, the microlithic assemblage was sufficiently large to form a useful basis for classification.

Over 90 microliths and micro-burins (and 60 cores) were discovered, and some of the assemblage seems to be linked with those from Wangford and from the Marsden district of the Pennines. Microlithic industries such as these were also in existence in the extreme south-west and north-east, in Wales, the Isle of Man and parts of Scotland. The Shippea Hill industry also agrees in some respects with the French Sauveterrian culture. Microlithic shapes found at Two Mile Bottom, on the other hand, echo some sort of social identification with groups in Lincolnshire and elsewhere.

The final phase of the Mesolithic, beginning about 6400 b.c., saw the dry Continental climate give way to warm, moist oceanic conditions. In the North Sea the water level continued to rise and warmth and rainfall stimulated the growth of deciduous forest which included oak, elm and, in particular, lime. The reindeer of the colder climes had long since disappeared.

It is possible at this stage that social development took place along more local lines; either that, or small groups flourished within the social structures of large groups. In any event the Wensum valley sites at Hellesdon, Sparham and Lyng, for example, can be attributed to this last (c 6500 to c 3500 b.c.) phase. Only the flint industries survive, and here core axes were still being produced.

5.

There is no evidence from East Anglia of burial customs, though several skeletons thought to be Mesolithic have been found and, in 1954, a skull on the banks of the River Yare at Strumpshaw. Precise dating, however, is difficult.

Although in terms of time the Mesolithic represents but a fragment compared to the vast bulk of the Palaeolithic, it did see far reaching advances, technical and social, and the development of new skills. The seasonal movements of the hunting groups – an understanding of which assists the classification of sites in terms of function, season, economy and environment – is only now being perceived.

However, the seas were beginning to close around the shores of Britain, divorcing it from Continental developments and delaying the major innovations that were to follow.

First Farmers (Neolithic)

In East Anglia the Neolithic (the New Stone Age) is now regarded as having lasted from c 3500 b.c. to c 2000 b.c., and it may conveniently be divided into two periods, Early and Late. Man clearly emerges during these periods as a major force in controlling the environment particularly through forest clearance – mainly in the chalk areas of eastern and southern England – and agricultural activities, even though many parts of the country were left virtually untouched.

At the start of the period the mean temperature is thought to have been slightly higher than that of today, though possibly declining to today's level by the end of the second millennium b.c. It may also have been slightly wetter. The sea stood at the approximate levels of today, although in the mid- to late third millennium a slightly higher sea level is indicated as the Fenland basin became covered by the sea, resulting in a thick deposit of clay.

One unusual phenomenon which has been detected in buried soils is a marked fall in elm pollen which evidently occurred in different places throughout Britain during the centuries before 3000 b.c. At first the reason was thought to have been climatic, but it is now considered that man, in some way, was to blame. He may have been chopping elm branches for fodder (as primitive farmers still do today) because extensive pasture did not exist in the largely forested terrain of the time. Another possibility is that an insect-borne fungus (perhaps akin to modern Dutch elm disease) was responsible. At Hockham Mere, for example, the elm decline took place as an isolated event, although here other trees were also reduced, the forest regenerating after a short time. Not until later did grasses, heather and other plants of the open country spread into the area as a result of widespread tree clearance.

However, Late Palaeolithic groups were still ekeing out an existence in East Anglia when the events which foreshadowed the Neolithic, and which were to revolutionise world economy and pave the way for the development of our present civilisation, first occurred in the Middle East.

As early as 9000 b.c. the inhabitants of Iran and the plains of the Middle East discovered how to cultivate cereals and domesticate sheep and goats. The implications were enormous. Not only did the augmented food supply enable larger populations than ever before to settle but it also, in part, dictated a more sedentary lifestyle which in turn allowed a richer culture to develop. Ultimately, the idea of food cultivation was carried to the Mesolithic peoples of Europe, the earliest farmers arriving in the Low Countries in the sixth millennium. Several hundred years were to pass, however, before these practices became widespread in England.

Radio-carbon dates suggest that the earliest agricultural communities crossed from the Continental landmass to the British Isles early in the fourth millennium b.c., bringing with them the seed corn, flocks and herds which were to establish the first Neolithic agrarian and agricultural economy in the country. It is likely that the first movements were by small communities, large scale settlements taking place once workable areas had been established. It is also possible that the first pioneers made this hazardous journey in skin boats carrying crew, animals, seed and supplies.

These first farmers also brought with them a tradition of stone (as opposed to flint) working and, perhaps even more useful in terms of study, a tradition of pottery making.

The arrival of a ceramic tradition is important. For the first time, and aside from flint and stone, here was a material which could be fashioned, designed or decorated according to individual or group tradition. Equally crucial, pottery is not so vulnerable (as is wood, for example) to soil acidity. In archaeological terms, it is the study of pottery which has contributed so much to our understanding of the peoples of these remote periods of time.

It is difficult to assess how immediate was the impact of the Neolithic farmers on those resident communities which were still following Meso-lithic traditions. It does not follow, for example, that Mesolithic hunters automatically turned to agricultural practices at the earliest opportunity. Indeed, the great labour involved in even elementary crop raising, as against hunting and gathering, may mean that some Mesolithic groups had little need or little desire to change their way of life. So the period of transition is hard to interpret. For example, it is possible that some Late Mesolithic flint industries are contemporary with the Early Neolithic. It is certainly difficult to distinguish between the two.

It can also be assumed that in the initial period after settlement all the efforts of the newcomers were concentrated on the production of food and work with herds. It would have left little time to devote to the construction of major monuments, sites or even substantial settlements. Indeed, it is likely that the earliest Neolithic monuments for which there are radio-carbon dates do not in fact reflect structures erected by the first, second or perhaps even third generations to settle here. A lengthy period of adjustment and settlement would have been necessary before communities could meet and collectively erect such structures as the megalithic tombs of the north and west, or the causewayed enclosures of southern and eastern England.

The first farmers are usually named from a type-site in Wiltshire as the Windmill Hill tradition, and a general settlement pattern suggests they had a marked preference for the chalk lands. Evidence is also accumulating to suggest that on the arrival of the first farmers the chalk lands supported thick oak forest, as the heavier clay soils did, so it may be presumed that the main attraction of the chalk areas was the light soil – easily tilled once cleared – and not, as previously supposed, a comparative freedom from trees.

In our region what slight traces we have of the Early Neolithic are found throughout the lighter soil areas, with a marked apparent avoidance of the heavier boulder clay of central East Anglia and the glacial sands of North Norfolk.

Little has been learned of the local houses of the period, but evidence elsewhere suggests that small rectangular timber framed buildings with, sometimes, stone wall footings may have been used. They would have disappeared long ago. Thus the principal remains of the Early Neolithic are flints and fragments of a plain, dark brown pottery of a surprisingly high quality.

The pottery forms most commonly found are bag shaped vessels and bowls, the best local examples coming from Broome Heath (Ditchingham) and from Cambridgeshire. Similar pottery has been found at a number of other sites including, for example, Sparham, Edingthorpe, Brettenham, Eaton Heath (Norwich) and Spong Hill (North Elmham).

Although the earliest pottery bowls are plain, decorated examples, known as Mildenhall ware, were in use in the later fourth millennium. A common type – found at Hurst Fen and Hayland House, Mildenhall, and at Eriswell – are bowls with a distinctive decoration. It is assumed that the use of Mildenhall ware was fairly widespread.

Hurst Fen inhabitants lived by cultivating emmer and barley and by keeping cattle, pigs, sheep and goats, although the evidence for these animals is slight as the acid soil conditions of the site were not conducive to the preservation of bone refuse. The presence of flint arrowheads suggests that they may have supplemented their diet by hunting. Some forest clearance presumably took place. Pottery at Hurst Fen, for some reason, may have been precious as some pots seem to have been repaired.

Flint, however, was still a vital raw material for weapons and tools including the most important, the hafted axe, the only tool available for tree-felling and forest clearance. Hundreds of these axes have been found in

East Anglia, usually isolated, so that precise dating is difficult. Their form, however, is distinctive. Core axeheads were chipped into shape and sometimes sharpened by polishing on a block of stone. Leaf shaped arrowheads are also common, while common tools include scrapers, knives, choppers and hammers. A wide variety of objects manufactured in wood may also be assumed; indeed, the timber trackways built across the marshlands of the Somerset Levels provide one indication of the standard of woodworking skills and woodland management already attained.

There is virtually no evidence for hunting on Early Neolithic sites. Instead, they grew cereals as well as herding cattle. Little is known, either, of the size and nature of the fields, but pollen analysis of samples from Hockham Mere has shown that plots were being cultivated – though in this case not for very long. The plots may have been abandoned as the soil value decreased.

Evidence of the use of ploughing comes from a few sites in Britain where furrows cut into the chalk bedrock were subsequently covered by earthworks, as at South Street in Wiltshire. One conclusion is that Neolithic ploughs may already have been drawn by pairs of oxen.

The newcomers seem to have arrived at Peacock's Farm (Shippea Hill) c 3400 b.c. (it was then, as in earlier Mesolithic times, a wooded area) bringing with them a tradition of pottery making, crop raising and animal husbandry. They proceeded to clear a small part of the surrounding woodland for agricultural purposes and conducted a subsistence economy. It is a familiar pattern reflected on sites in other parts of the British Isles. Occupation at Peacock's Farm, however, was by no means continuous from Mesolithic to Neolithic, and indeed, radio-carbon dating has suggested a gap of over a thousand years between the two phases. The site at Broome Heath may also have been inhabited intermittently, perhaps over a period of 1500 years, a broad sweep of time throughout which the style of the pottery hardly changed.

Other than isolated finds of human bones, which may indicate casual rather than formal burial, there is slight evidence in Norfolk of burial traditions aside from long mounds or barrows. These have been identified at West Rudham, Harpley Common, Broome Heath and Felthorpe, while the ploughed remnants of other possible examples have been detected from the air.

Windmill Hill style pottery has been found on the surface of the long barrow at Broome Heath identical to the adjacent settlement, and at Harpley, but only that at West Rudham has been excavated. No groups of inhumations were found inside the mound, which is 65m long and 18m wide, but evidence of burning was found on a platform of gravel, presumably a pyre, which had been subsequently covered with turf and more gravel. Similar materials were used to cover a ditch-encircled area to the south.

A mound at Worlington (Suffolk) forms the eccentric core of a later (Bronze Age) round barrow called Swale's Tumulus. In the original mound signs of an extensive fire and cremated bones suggest a pyre; north of the mound a grave contained charred oak boards with cremated bone fragments, burnt flints, potsherds and parts of a polished flint axe-head. However, the Worlington mound is an isolated example of Neolithic cremation in the region and an unusual succession of Neolithic and Bronze Age burials.

From the limited number of long barrows it is deduced that only a small proportion of the Neolithic population was entitled to burial beneath these imposing monuments. We can only speculate how they disposed of the majority of the dead.

Causewayed camps (enclosures bounded by one or more concentric interrupted or 'causewayed' ditches, frequently on hill-top sites) also belong to this Early period. Windmill Hill, after which the ceramic tradition is named, is a fine example. Two sites discovered by aerial photography at Hainford and Roughton are the only possible examples of this type of enclosure in Norfolk.

The camps, which vary widely in size and complexity, seem in general to have been laid out with regard to the topography, but the form of their ditches makes it unlikely they were solely for defence. One suggestion is that they may have served as cattle kraals. Another suggestion is that they may be regarded as regional centres or meeting places, rather as the Medieval fairs.

At Eaton Heath (Norwich) evidence was found – including flints and pottery – of a Neolithic settlement overlaid by ditch systems of Late Pre-Roman Iron Age and the first century AD. The site also produced a series of curious shafts of unknown use, over 40 shallow pits and 16 (probable) post-holes. The 21 shafts of the late third millennium had been dug into soft sands and gravel and provided with clay linings. They varied between 1m and 2m in diameter, were as deep as 8m, and they occur in what appears to be a domestic context. Similar shafts are better known in Romano/Celtic religious contexts, and their occurrence on Eaton Heath at such an early date has aroused considerable interest.

If the Early Neolithic is something of a puzzle the Late phase is even more so, for there are signs of no less than four pottery traditions – bowl, and three new groups, grooved ware, Peterborough and beaker. However, although pottery has been found at a number of sites, even during excavation, no substantial building remains have been found which might indicate the style of the settlements. The flint industries associated with these sites display a cruder and perhaps less refined workmanship than the Early Neolithic.

The Late Neolithic bowl tradition is characterised by pottery known as Peterborough ware, a coarse, usually round based pottery with thickened

Fig 7. *Pottery and Tools of the Neolithic.* From top to bottom the pots are: a decorated bowl from Hurst Fen, Mildenhall and a plain bowl from Broome Heath, Ditchingham both late fourth millennium b.c.; Grooved Ware vessels from Spong Hill, North Elmham and Thetford and a Peterborough Tradition bowl from Spong Hill with a Grooved Ware dish from Feltwell, all of the late third millenium b.c. The tools include an antler pick (top right), a hafted polished stone axe (centre), arrows and bone needles.

rims and profuse decoration, produced by impressing a twisted cord, a fingernail or the leg-bone of a bird. The type is distributed all over southern England, more sparsely in East Anglia, though sites do occur in Breckland (including Grimes Graves), Ickburgh, Witton, Brancaster, Spong Hill, Eaton and Broome Heath. It has also been found at Edingthorpe lying in a hollow which may have been part of a habitation.

Another tradition also produced distinctive pottery, grooved ware (previously known as Rinyo-Clacton), and examples have been found at West Runton, Edingthorpe, Hunstanton, Spong Hill, Grimes Graves and Thetford. At Honington the users of this pottery may have lived in oval huts with pits outside. At Hunstanton was a 'corral' in which pigs, rather than cattle, were probably kept.

One henge monument (a circular enclosure defined by a ditch and usually an external bank, with one or more entrances and sometimes with post or stone settings within) has been discovered by aerial photography at Arminghall. Subsequent radio-carbon analysis of charcoal from the post setting suggested a date of around 2500 b.c. The secondary silting of the inner ditch contained quantities of Iron Age sherds and Roman pottery and coins.

The nature of the rites (it is tempting to deduce a religious or ceremonial use, though it may not necessarily be accurate to do so) can only be surmised.

The Arminghall henge monument is set on a terrace of the River Tas with the remains of at least twelve later round barrows nearby. The henge consists of two concentric ditches with a low earthen bank (15m wide) between them. The inner ditch (8.5m wide and 2.3m deep) has a single causeway on the south-west. Excavations in 1935 revealed eight substantial post-holes in a horseshoe shaped setting, irregularly spaced, within the central area. It would seem the oak posts stood at least 2.5m above the original ground.

About 1900 b.c. the beaker pottery tradition arrived, and the characteristic pot of their tradition is a thin, well made 'beaker' of shallow S-profile, ornamented either by hyphenated horizontal lines formed by impressing a comb or twisted cord. The ornamentation is frequently in geometric patterns.

Beakers offer one of the best examples in prehistory of the arrival of a new technique from the Continent. Although this style of pottery is found throughout Western Europe the closest parallels to the earliest British beakers are in the Rhineland; thus the immediate source of this innovating technique is apparent. Most beakers from East Anglia are isolated finds, some probably for domestic use, though the majority probably come from inhumation graves in which soil acidity has destroyed the skeletal remains. Others have been discovered accompanying burials beneath round barrows, a type of monument that replaced the long-used long barrows.

Within these round barrows bodies were regularly buried in a flexed position.

Inhumations and cremations have been found. Some were interred beneath round barrows while others were placed in isolated graves apparently unmarked on the surface. Occasionally, as at Mildenhall, human bones are found scattered in refuse pits. Four pits dug for inhumation burials were found at Trowse in the centre of a barrow. However, the number and distribution of beaker barrows is no real clue as to the size of the local population for, as with Early Neolithic barrows, it is clear that not everyone was buried in this way.

A principal weapon of the beaker people – as in earlier periods – was the bow. Stone wrist guards, to protect the archer's wrist from the recoil of the bow string, have been found at several places, including Brandon, along with a flint arrowhead, axe hammers, daggers and polished knives. Again, little is known of beaker users' settlements, but it is possible these were homesteads suited to stock breeding activities. From the evidence of Lakenheath, Edingthorpe and Mildenhall, they seem to have been herdsmen who supplemented their supplies by fishing, fowling and cultivation.

It does seem, however, that the population increased in the Late Neolithic, for it became necessary to expand areas required for cultivation and grazing. In the Breckland this led to the clearance of some of the deciduous woodland, as the type of farming practised by the Windmill Hill people quickly exhausted the thin soils. As before, trees were felled with flint or stone axes and the stumps probably burned. An analysis of pollen from the lake mud at Hockham Mere shows a great expansion of the pollen derived from grasses, ling and herbs, and although the clearance roughly corresponds with the Late phase it follows a regeneration of the forest after the initial temporary clearance of the Early Neolithic. The presence of agricultural weeds such as ribwort plantain also underlines an extension of farming practices. The regeneration of woodland would also have been hampered by the grazing of domestic animals. The end result, of course, was the creation of the Breckland heaths.

Trade also owed its expansion to the people of the Late Neolithic. It is not really certain when trade in, for example, stone axes began, but by the first quarter of the third millennium b.c. they were being brought from Great Langdale to Norfolk while Cornish axes were reaching the Ipswich region and the Essex coast.

As far as stone (as opposed to flint) implements are concerned one means by which evidence of the source of the stone can be obtained is to examine the material used. This is done by cutting a thin slice from an axe, mounting it on glass and grinding it down until a light will pass through it. The specimen is then studied under a special microscope so that the crystal structures can be ascertained and comparisons made with samples from known sources, such as the Lake District, Wales or Cornwall. In this way sources of different rocks used for axes can be accurately identified and distribution patterns established.

It also seems that the first systematic exploitation of this area's flint resources, by mining into chalk, was by people using plain bowls, grooved ware and the Peterborough tradition pottery of the Late Neolithic. The complex at Grimes Graves – which has a date of c 2100 b.c. through to c 1800 b.c. for the galleried shafts, and to c 1600 b.c. for the shallow pits – owes its prestige not only to its size but also to the extent to which it has been excavated. The site covers some 90 acres, and over 350 shafts have been identified. Other mines in Norfolk have been found at Buckenham Tofts, Lynford, Great Massingham, Whitlingham and Ringland.

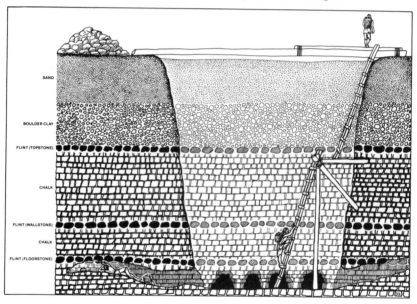

Fig 8. *Diagrammatic Section of a Flint Mine at Grimes Graves, near Brandon.* A vertical shaft was sunk through the chalk and overlying sand and shattered chalk to reach the best flint. Although several seams of flint occur at Grimes Graves only the best (the 'floorstone') was extensively mined from galleries which radiated out from the shaft. Some mines at Grimes Graves are more than 12m deep.

As far as Grimes Graves is concerned the busiest period seems to have occurred c 2000 b.c. The mines range from opencast pits 3m to 4.5m deep, to shafts cut through the sand and chalk to a depth of 12m with radiating galleries linking one with another. As each pit was excavated so the waste material was dumped in pits previously exhausted. Polished axes and the antlers of red deer, used as levers, have been found in the mines, while tools made from the shoulder and leg-bones of oxen also occur.

The risk of death or injury from suffocation or material collapse must have been considerable. Other than a physical danger there was also the possibility that a shaft, which might have taken weeks to excavate, could be barren of suitable flint. 'Better luck next time' is a sentiment which is often attached to a curious and unexpectedly exotic group of chalk artefacts, including a figurine, discovered some years ago during the excavation of pit 15. However, the authenticity of this is doubted by many.

Around the shafts were also working floors on which the knappers trimmed the flint nodules into the shape of axes which, possibly, were traded unfinished from the mine. The distribution patterns of these factory products will produce much information, and a programme of flint analysis has already started under the auspices of the British Museum. At the time of writing, however, the results have not emerged.

No houses for the Grimes Graves miners have been detected, and the lack of an obvious water supply is often noted, too. However, the site is not very far from the River Thet, and it is interesting that a pit excavated in 1971 is now full of water.

The work seems to have occupied a handful of miners over a number of centuries, so there may not have been a permanent occupation of the site. If the complex did employ specialist bands of miners and knappers then they may represent groups of craftsmen who could only have been supported from a surplus of agricultural produce. Indeed, they may have depended for their food and supplies of antler picks on local farmer groups.

It has also been estimated that over 50,000 antlers (the vast majority of them shed antlers) were used in the mines, which presupposes either a plentiful deer population in the surrounding woodland and a sufficient number of people to gather the antlers, or imports from other areas. A somewhat casual attitude to death might be indicated by the use of a human femur as a lever and by the discovery in other shafts of a girl's skeleton and fragments of human bones. On the other hand they may represent a disturbed burial.

What seems to have been a fairly stable economy until the mid-third millennium also seems to have come to an abrupt and puzzling end. At least, tree clearance stopped, and it may have heralded some sort of prehistoric recession. The precise reasons for this major upheaval are not clear.

By the time the Neolithic had drawn to a close, however, Norfolk was occupied by the progeny of many native cultures, identified from the last remaining plain bowl tradition and the decorated Peterborough tradition, mingled with the progeny of immigrants from the Continent clearly identified from beakers. More important still, East Anglia, from being a land of hunters was now firmly established as a region of stock breeders and farmers.

Metal Smiths (Bronze Age)

The Bronze Age, now generally dated c 2000 to c 650 b.c., may be divided into three phases, Early, Middle and Late

Much of our knowledge of the period is derived from burial and ritual sites and unassociated artefacts, which tends to give an uneven picture much concerned with matters sepulchral and technological and not enough about more mundane matters. Thus while some aspects of the Bronze Age (material possessions, for example) are well explained, other facets of life (settlements, dwellings) are still substantial blanks.

The climate of the second millennium was probably drier than that before or after. The environment of the chalk areas remained open with much grassland, and there is evidence from several sites in England of wind-blown silt deriving from dry, broken ground. During the Early period elm was still at a low level, but ash and birch show an increase. The period from 1200 b.c., however, is marked by an increase in rainfall and a decline of temperatures. It seems likely that in some upland areas the field systems were abandoned – perhaps because the shorter, cooler and wetter summers gave insufficient time for crops to ripen – which in turn suggests a general shift from cereal farming to stock rearing.

Just as the Neolithic opened with the arrival on these shores of ideas of enormous importance (cultivation, and the domestication of animals), so the Bronze Age heralded a substantial technological leap forward.

Metallurgy – the smelting of ore and the casting of tools and weapons – began, like farming, in the Middle East and spread slowly into western Europe. The early metal workers discovered, after initially using copper, that by adding one part tin to nine parts copper they could produce tools and weapons infinitely superior to those of copper alone. Copper is a soft metal with a brittle cutting edge. Bronze is considerably more durable than either stone or flint. Moreover, the casting method allowed a far greater flexibility in design.

East Anglia, however, has no natural resources of copper or tin and it follows that the earliest objects or ingots must have been imported. Indeed, much of it seems to have come from Ireland and Cornwall. Even so, the introduction of this new metal seems to have been slow, and it could be that the early possession of it was something of a status symbol confined to the wealthier elements of society. Its spread into wider use only began when an adequate supply of materials, perhaps added to by the melting down of obsolete tools and weapons, became available to those who possessed the necessary technical skills.

Some cultural traditions clearly survived from the final phase of the Neolithic, among them the beaker people who were associated with copper at an early stage. Copper was certainly in use before the end of the Neolithic, and copper flat axes, for example, from Hardingham, West

Fig 9. *Early Bronze Age Pottery and Implements.* The pottery traditions illustrated are beakers (right, from Rollesby and the handled example, bottom, from Bodney Hall), food vessel (left, from Feltwell) and collared urn (top, from Witton). All are dated to the earlier second millennium b.c. Although simple bronze implements were being produced at this time, flint and stone were the principal raw materials for tools. The bronze flanged axe from Swaffham and tanged spearhead from Weeting (bottom left) are shown unhafted, as this is how they are found today. Characteristic flints of this period include barbed and tanged arrowheads (left) and dagger blades (bottom left, from Tottenhoe), while stone from the Whin Sill of Northumberland was used for axe-hammers (bottom right, also from Tottenhoe).

35

Runton and Horning, suggest early importations into the area. Indeed, the arrival of the beaker tradition is looked upon as a watershed in British prehistory, marking a major social and economic change. In spite of the warlike nature of some of their grave goods, however, there is no evidence of the establishment of a beaker autocracy over the indigenous population. Materials from sites such as henges in fact suggest an intermingling of various traditions or groups of newcomers and natives in the Late Neolithic.

A number of ceramic traditions can be identified in the early second millennium. The 'food vessel' tradition, descended from the Peterborough tradition, persisted longer than the beaker. The largest concentration of English food vessels lies in Yorkshire, and the pottery form is a coarse, thick walled and decorated bowl. It is fairly rare in East Anglia, though pottery from Feltwell and Shouldham suggests that the tradition at least spread as far as Breckland. Other pots from Needham (Suffolk), Swannington and Wereham, though similar, may represent later local developments.

The limited number of burials with food vessels and their usual accoutrements also suggests that the local spread of the tradition was small. Food vessels were placed with the dead at Warren Hill (Mildenhall), but another distinctive type was sometimes used to accompany or contain cremated remains. Known as collared urns, they are found fairly frequently.

It does seem that the activities of the people employing the food vessel tradition in East Anglia were largely confined to parts of Norfolk and north west Suffolk. The people of this period seem to have had a fairly settled economy. From Fengate (Peterborough) comes evidence of effective land management, while at Plantation Farm (Shippea Hill), where they lived on a sandy ridge surrounded by alder swamp, they practised a mixed farming economy.

Commercial interests, however, were increasing, and imported bronzes are scattered over the light soil areas of Norfolk, though they are most common in Breckland and in Cambridgeshire. The chief tool brought to East Anglia, probably initially from Ireland, was the flat axe-head. Rare halberds, awls and knife-daggers with Continental prototypes, have been recorded, too. Trade with Scandinavia is indicated by distinctive flint dagger-blades also found in Breckland.

Wessex lay across the trade routes from Ireland to the Continent, and about 1600 b.c. one particular rank in their society seems to have grown wealthy from international commerce. How wealthy, and by what precise means, is not wholly clear, but a distinctive group of burials with rich grave goods identifies one group of people.

A third building stage of Stonehenge, for example, raises the possibility of some form of centralised political authority to command the necessary resources for its construction – the welding together of separate social or tribal units of Wessex into a single larger territory – while it has also been suggested that an increasing development of pastoralism would be much more likely to give rise to a stratified warrior society than an economy based on cereal production or mixed farming.

Wessex influence in this area may be glimpsed from one rich and elaborate interment at Little Cressingham. Some distinctive burial mounds may also belong to this phase. In any event the local imports, including bronze axes, awls and ornaments of gold, were substantial. They also included amber, bronze pins and daggers, possibly from mainland Europe; and faience beads, possibly from Egypt.

Locally their barrows, normally surrounded by a ditch with an external bank sometimes as much as 55m in diameter, can be recognised at Rushford (Brettenham), Great Bircham, West Rudham and Weasenhall All Saints. Two main types, 'bell' and 'disc', may be discerned. 'Disc' barrows (many of which may have been lost, for being small they fall easy prey to the plough) have been identified at Wellingham, Rushford and Salthouse. It has been suggested that 'bell' barrows contain male cremations or inhumations, while 'disc' barrows were erected over cremated females.

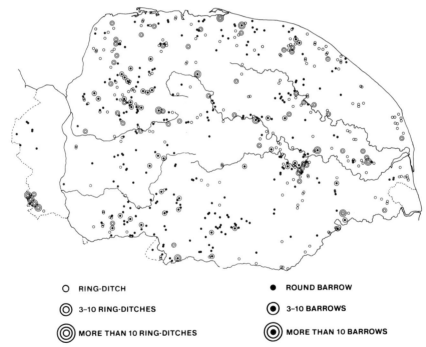

O   RING-DITCH   ●   ROUND BARROW

◎   3–10 RING-DITCHES   ◉   3–10 BARROWS

◎   MORE THAN 10 RING-DITCHES   ◉   MORE THAN 10 BARROWS

Fig 10. *The Distribution of Round Barrows in Norfolk.* This map records not only the upstanding mounds, but also remnants of others discovered from aerial photographs and generally referred to as 'ring-ditches'.

There is little evidence, however, to substantiate the hypothesis.

A 'bell' barrow at Great Bircham was found to contain an inverted urn with cremated bones, a bronze awl and gold covered beads. The body of a male at Little Cressingham had with it a bronze dagger with a wooden hilt, a flat dagger, a necklace of amber beads, a thin rectangular gold plate and other sheet gold mountings. In 1849, when the barrow was removed for agricultural purposes, the skull, remarkable for its thickness, was said to contain a brain which 'had an average share of the intellectual portion in addition to a large development of that portion said to be the seat of the animal passions ...'

Another Little Cressingham round barrow (c 1690 b.c.) was excavated more recently. There was no sign of a grave, but studies showed the site was open grassland when the barrow was built. The post-glacial primeval forest was long gone, and indeed, there was evidence of arable land use in the vicinity.

In Norfolk the most common prehistoric earthworks still to be seen today are round barrows. At the time of writing the sites of 625 barrows (a majority of them probably Early Bronze Age) are known in the county, and the remains of 800 more are suspected following the examination of aerial photographs, most of them in the Breckland and Goodsand and Loam areas. Some were evidently re-built and enlarged.

About 1400 b.c., and during the Middle Bronze Age, the pottery became less sophisticated, degenerating into simple urns which, in Norfolk, persisted until the end of the Bronze Age. The pots are usually large, ill-fired urns of coarse clay, chiefly known as receptacles for cremated remains. This new pottery style is best seen in southern England where it is associated with a new burial tradition.

It is referred to as the Deverel-Rimbury tradition (named after the sites of two characteristic cemeteries), the new tradition being the placing of many urned cremations in a cemetery, or 'urnfield'. Although this pottery is only rarely found in Norfolk (only five cremation cemeteries are known), prodigious finds have been made in Essex, at Ardleigh, where the pots have been decorated in a distinctive local manner.

A few burials of the Late phase are known, and some cinerary urns similar to those from barrows have been found without a trace of a mound at, for example, Rockland St. Andrew and Needham. The custom of barrow building, it would seem, was obsolete among some groups, though its persistence elsewhere is shown by the construction at Salthouse Heath of tiny mounds only a few feet in diameter, each with an urn containing cremated bones. The adoption of urnfield burial and the cessation of providing the dead with possessions implies innovations in beliefs and religious practices.

The only local settlement at which urns have been recognised is at Mildenhall. However, elsewhere, as in Sussex, small farmsteads with groups of round huts, attendant fields and cemeteries have been found. Like their ancestors, the people of the urn tradition seem to have been pastoralists who supplemented the products of their flocks by cultivation. Outside Norfolk they are known mainly from the contents of the round barrows which they erected, or enlarged, to contain the cremated remains of their dead.

It would not seem unreasonable to assume that metalwork, especially a hoard, was lost or concealed close to rather than in a settlement – though hoards have been found on settlements elsewhere in southern England. In a few areas of Norfolk concentrations of bronze finds are particularly marked, though settlements have not been identified. One such concentration is between the rivers Little Ouse and Wissey, where the chalk escarpment abuts directly on the Fens; another is further north on the high chalkland between the rivers Ingol and Heacham. Two factors which might have influenced the siting of a smithy are the availability of wood (for charcoal) and nearby settlements or routes used by potential customers.

Evidence for the development of a substantial local bronze industry can be inferred from the large number of hoards or caches of tools and weapons presumably concealed and never recovered. Over 80 Middle and Late Bronze Age hoards have been found in Norfolk, and in all 560 find-spots of Bronze Age metalwork have been recorded. It amounts to a vast quantity of metalwork.

The reason for so many hoards is not wholly clear, but it is presumed that the smiths, perhaps 'working' a particular area or route, buried parts of their stock with the intention of collecting it the next time they were in the vicinity. With the introduction of iron, however, bronze became obsolete. It seems possible, therefore, that in the Late Bronze Age the smiths had little reason to try to recover their largely redundant stocks. Hoards seem to comprise the possessions of one individual or the stock-in-trade of itinerant smiths who presumably derived the bulk of their raw material from obsolete, damaged or discarded weapons and tools. The chief products are axes (with loops for securing to the haft), but a wide variety of implements, including spearheads, were produced.

The native smiths also produced palstaves, bracelets, finger rings, pins and those well-known ornaments of fashion, torcs. Occasionally they also

Fig 11 (over). *Reconstruction of a Bronze Age Farmstead about 1000 b.c.* Small groups of thatched round houses were surrounded by a palisade and set amongst well ordered fields. Some fields were ploughed whilst others were given over to the grazing of herds and flocks. Extensive woodland still existed although some of the areas cleared during earlier periods had become heaths. Frequently the earlier round barrows which had been sited on these heaths were re-used by later Bronze Age groups. The farmsteads, within which the everyday duties of food preparation and the manufacture of clothing took place, were visited by bronze smiths or salesmen selling the latest fashions in tools and weapons. Broken and old-fashioned tools would, in part, have been traded against new bronzes and expensive gold jewellery.

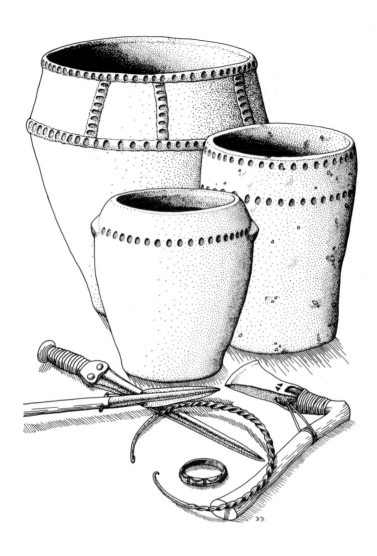

Fig 12. *Middle Bronze Age Pottery and Bronzes.* The pottery urns which we often find containing the cremated remains of the dead are from (top to bottom) Needham, Shouldham and Bergh Apton. The commonest tool of the period was an axe or 'palstave' (right, from Hunstanton). Weapons included spears (centre, from Stibbard) and rapiers (left, Swaffham), while ornaments included torcs worn around the neck and bracelets (centre bottom, from Hunstanton).

made sickles for the farmers and saws, chisels and gouges for the carpenters, who in turn built wooden containers and even boats. Many varieties of weapon were also produced including, in the Late Bronze Age, leaf-shaped slashing swords.

Some items of bronze equipment are undoubtedly of foreign origin, perhaps due to the arrival in Britain of alien smiths or the copying of traded imports, but other tools and weapons display a continuity of native tradition. That redundant materials were re-used becomes clear from a large number of hoards which comprise in part lumps of metal and broken pieces of equipment, together with the newly cast and unfinished tools and weapons.

Examples of Late Bronze Age hoards include a site at Snettisham which contained socketed axes, sword fragments, molten scrap bronze and the hilt of an imported dagger. Another hoard of over one hundred items was found at Gorleston in 1952. Yet another large hoard from Beeston Regis contained, unusually, fragments of a pottery vessel, and remarkably, pieces of string made of nettle fibres and lime tree bark.

The appearance of both weapons and 'horsey' gear (harness, wagon fittings) is indicative of a stratified warrior society in which bronze industries may have been centrally controlled. A growth of military activity and a large number of efficient weapons is matched by the evolution of defended settlements which eventually become formidable hill-forts. An early example is Rams Hill (Berkshire), an enclosed settlement on the edge of the chalk. Investigations here revealed a pre-Iron Age sequence of defences including a stone-faced rampart, timber revetting and palisade, and a timber entrance. Occupation seems to have been intermittent (perhaps seasonal) and the economy largely pastoral, with cattle predominating.

Population increase and climatic decline created an apparent increase in pastoralism, as marked by extensive ditch systems; social tension, perhaps, led to raiding, and the resulting need to defend one's herd and grain supplies.

To the last century of the Bronze Age must be attributed the winged shapes of sword scabbards found at Lakenheath, and these, and other Continental bronzes, seem to provide the prelude to the Iron Age. It was a period of transition which may have been witnessed, for example, by the people of West Harling (Micklemoor Hill).

Before leaving the Bronze Age it is important not to let the great abundance of metal equipment obscure the significance of the gradual development of land management with mixed farming, the use of the horse and wheeled vehicles, and in general a more developed society. Cultivation of the heavier loams presumably produced an increasing yield of cereal crops, and the systematic herding of cattle and the grazing of sheep must also have improved the stock.

Fig 13. *Pots and Bronzes of the Late Bronze Age and the Start of the Iron Age.* The pottery bowl on the left was found at Beeston Regis with many Late Bronze Age objects in it. The tall jar (right) and delicate bowl (bottom left) are from the early Iron Age settlement at West Harling. By this time the range of bronze implements being cast was large and included specialists' tool kits such as the carpenter's chisels and gouges (right) from Carleton Rode. Efficient swords (centre, from Weston Longville) had been introduced and the spear (bottom, from Southery) was still common.

The coming of Iron

About 650 b.c. a knowledge of the use of iron reached these shores. It was a technique which had already been in general use in central Europe for at least 300 years.

In Britain the processes of production have left little trace, and few furnaces for iron smelting have been found. Other signs of iron working, such as slag and cinders, have been found more widely on settlement sites. Bronze undoubtedly survived into the period – indeed, it was retained for some time, particularly for ornamental or decorative items – but iron became the predominant material. Low grade iron ores, it should be remembered, were available locally, at least, from the gravel and Greensand deposits.

In the general absence of iron objects, however, the presence of the Early Iron Age communities is chiefly indicated by domestic pottery, mainly bowls and jars. The earliest iron using culture in Britain clearly derives from a Continental culture known as Late Halstatt (named after an important site in Austria), and variations in pottery and decoration enable us to identify distinct groups sharing a similar background. Late Halstatt pottery can be compared with Late Neolithic beakers in that the tradition witnessed a technological change, in this later case from bronze to iron.

Settlers in Breckland seem closely related to communities around the Fenland basin in Cambridgeshire and Northamptonshire, though the Fens at this time were uninhabitable because of a rise in the sea level. There was also sporadic settlement along the North Norfolk coast at Stiffkey, Cromer and Paston. The chief surviving features of these farmsteads are ditches, pits or post-holes.

The Early phase of the Iron Age in our area, however, is named after a site at West Harling (Micklemoor Hill). The pottery tradition is distinctive but tools, alas, are absent. Iron, of course, tends to rust, and it does not attract the attention of the casual searcher in quite the same way as bronze.

The West Harling settlement was built by farmers using the Halstatt-inspired pottery probably before 600 b.c. on a glacial knoll close to the River Thet. The identified features include a circular bank and shallow ditch with two causeways, within which were numerous pits and post-holes, probably representing a circular building; another circular setting of post-holes in an irregular oval enclosure defined by a shallow ditch; and an irregular rectilinear enclosure again defined by a shallow ditch.

It is likely that the major bank was an integral part of the house, but the roofing of the complete area would have presented many structural problems. One reconstruction suggests that the house was penannular in shape with an entrance on the west to an internal circular yard. The ridge roof would then have drained into this and into the external ditch, which also served as a refuse tip.

Inside the southern enclosure were traces of a rectangular building at least 8.25m long and built with sleeper beams into which vertical posts may have been set. This shape may have been an innovation introduced by foreign builders. The third smaller building may have had a conical roof.

The people of West Harling herded oxen and sheep, cultivated wheat and hunted wild pig, red deer, the crane and the beaver. They made pottery (the remains of at least 530 pots were found in the ditch around the eastern house) and produced yarn. Domestic weaving, which had been known for hundreds of years, is also suggested by the discovery of triangular clay loom weights at other farmsteads.

The pottery – much more sophisticated than most preceeding examples, and the best Early Iron Age assemblage in East Anglia – consists of bowls and jars decorated with rows of finger-tip impressions or diagonal slashings on the rims. Hearths of cracked flint, hollows of various shapes, and runnels, were also detected.

Little is known of the burial customs of the Early Iron Age. Pottery has been found in barrows but Stiffkey, for example, contained no human remains; while pottery from a Weeting site may not be associated with the cremated bones also found there. It is not even certain if the barrows are of the same age as the pottery.

Although rectangular buildings were being erected elsewhere (Ricking-hall Inferior, Snarehill) a hearth of fired flints, a group of refuse pits, potsherds or animal bones, is often all that can now be detected of the farms.

This backward glance at the Early Iron Age provides a convenient point at which to end our prehistoric journey, which has taken us through 500,000 years; and although, during this period, by modern standards the level of technology does not seem to have been very high, the achievements nevertheless formed a basis for present-day society.

Warning

Reference to or representation of a site should not be taken as evidence that such a site may be visited. In almost every case sites are on private land. If permission to view is obtained it is of the utmost importance that sites, and crops and soils covering or surrounding them, should not be disturbed in any way.

Places to visit

Norwich Castle Museum, Castle Meadow, Norwich (Norwich 611277)
Yarmouth Museum, 4 South Quay (Yarmouth 55746)
King's Lynn Museum, Old Market Street (King's Lynn 5001)
Thetford Ancient House Museum, White Hart Street (Thetford 2599)
Grimes Graves, Weeting

Metal detectors

Found objects, other than those of gold and silver, belong to the owner of the land and not to the tenant or finder. Gold and silver objects are subject to a Treasure Trove inquest and must be reported to the local Coroner, though this can be done for you by the local museum. It is important to remember that all land belongs to someone, and prior permission to use a metal detector is thus required. Metal detector users are encouraged to report their finds to the Norfolk Museums Service so that objects of interest can be recorded. Sensible use of metal detectors is to be welcomed, and a pamphlet ('Archaeological Finds: Some Suggestions about the Use of Metal Detectors in Norfolk and Suffolk') has been compiled by the Scole Archaeological Committee. Copies are available from the Norfolk Archaeological Unit, Union House, Gressenhall, East Dereham. In addition a number of special clubs for detector users have been formed. Ask the Unit for details.

Organisations to join

Norfolk and Norwich Archaeological Society, Garsett House, St. Andrews Hall Plain, Norwich, NR3 1AT
Great Yarmouth and District Archaeological Society, c/o Central Library, Great Yarmouth
West Norfolk and King's Lynn Archaeological Society, c/o King's Lynn Museum, King's Lynn
Norfolk Industrial Archaeology Society, c/o the Bridewell Museum, Norwich
Norfolk Archaeological Rescue Group, c/o Norfolk Archaeological Unit, Union House, Gressenhall, East Dereham, NR20 4DR

(A list of other local societies is usually available from the Information Service, Norwich Central Library, Bethel Street, Norwich).

Index

Place-names are in Norfolk unless otherwise stated.